Volume 3: The Day of the Dinosaurs

BUT I'M NOT A DINOSAUR!

ME, NEITHER!

I AM! UM ... I THINK?

DINOSAUR? WHAT'S A DINOSAUR?

Written by
Jacqui Bailey

Illustrated by
Matthew Lilly

Kids Can Press

For Chris — my favorite
species of dinosaur
J. B.
For my dad
M. L.

With thanks to
Dr. Angela Milner of
The Natural History Museum,
London

Published in Canada by   Published in the U.S. by
Kids Can Press Ltd.   Kids Can Press Ltd.
29 Birch Avenue   2250 Military Road
Toronto, ON M4V 1E2   Tonawanda, NY 14150

www.kidscanpress.com

Printed in Hong Kong by
Wing King Tong Company Limited

The hardcover edition of this book
is smyth sewn casebound.

The paperback edition of this book is
limp sewn with a drawn-on cover.

CM 01 0 9 8 7 6 5 4 3 2 1
CM PA 01 0 9 8 7 6 5 4 3 2 1

Canadian Cataloguing in Publication Data

Bailey, Jacqui
The day of the dinosaur
(The cartoon history of the earth ; 3)
Includes index.

ISBN 1-55337-073-2 (bound)
ISBN 1-55337-082-1 (pbk.)

1. Dinosaurs – Comic books, strips,
etc. – Juvenile literature.
I. Lilly, Matthew.
II. Title. III. Series: Bailey, Jacqui.
Cartoon history of the earth ; 3.

QE861.5.B34 2001   j567.9
C00-933322-3

Kids Can Press is a Nelvana company

As you read this book, you'll see some words in capital letters — **LIKE THIS**. These words are listed in the Glossary on pages 30–31, where there is more information about them. And when you see the asterisk (✹), look for a box on the page that also has an asterisk. This box gives you even more information on the topic.

The Earth of 245 million years ago was strangely empty. Something so catastrophic had happened that more than half of all the different types of plants and animals in the world had vanished forever!

When a whole lot of plant and animal SPECIES die out at about the same time, scientists say there has been a "mass extinction."

The mass extinction of 245 million years ago was the biggest the world has ever known, but we still don't know what caused it. (It took about six million years to happen, mind you, so whatever the cause was, it was pretty slow.)

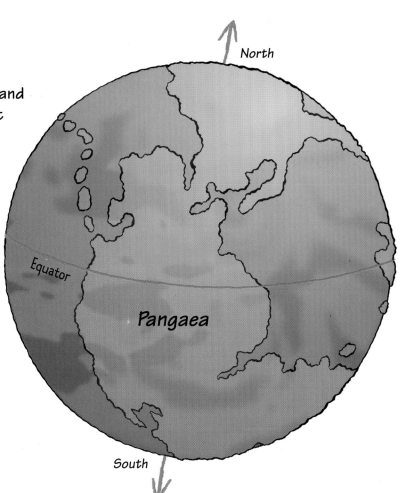

Lots of people think it had something to do with the movement of the land masses. Over hundreds of millions of years, the CONTINENTS had drifted closer and closer together until they became one enormous land mass, known as Pangaea. This changed the level of the sea, making it saltier, and caused huge climate changes. Many life-forms just couldn't cope.

But some survived. Ammonites with curved shells as big as car wheels still floated in the oceans.✱ Sharks and bony fish still hunted in the seas.

And slowly, over the next 20 million years or so, new types of animals and plants appeared ...

✱ Ammonites were **MOLLUSKS.** By about 65 million years ago, the shelled species had all died out. All except one. It's called the Nautilus, and it still swims in the Pacific Ocean today.

REPTILES took to the seas. Placodonts lumbered over rocky seabeds grinding up shellfish with their hard, stumpy teeth.

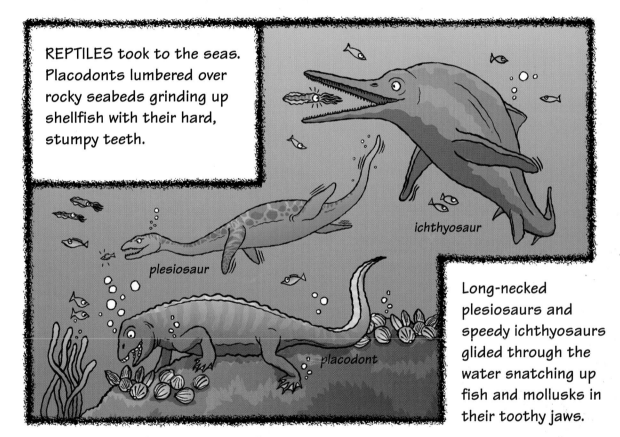

ichthyosaur

plesiosaur

placodont

Long-necked plesiosaurs and speedy ichthyosaurs glided through the water snatching up fish and mollusks in their toothy jaws.

And there was a strange-looking reptile called *Tanystropheus* that loved to eat fish but probably wasn't much of a swimmer.

Instead, we think it sat on the seashore and "fished" — using its long, snaky neck to reach deep into the water.

Rainstorms soaked the northern and southern coasts of Pangaea,
but in the center of this great continent it was hot and dry.

Lots of ARTHROPODS had survived the mass extinction — spiders, scorpions, millipedes, mites, centipedes and dragonflies.

And more species soon joined them. Creatures such as grasshoppers, stick insects and beetles.

Lots of AMPHIBIANS had died out, but now a whole lot of new kinds appeared on the scene, including the first frogs.

I DON'T KNOW, GLADYS. THIS PLACE JUST *ISN'T* THE SAME AS IT USED TO BE.

CRUNCH!

Ferns covered the ground in many places, and there were forests of CONIFER trees. Conifers, such as redwoods and pines, are sturdy plants that can survive in harsh conditions when they have to.

Herds of tubby, tusked reptiles, called dicynodonts, chewed on these tough plants (grass hadn't appeared yet). While other HERBIVORES, such as Lystrosaurus, squelched around in lakes and mud pools eating water plants.

They were all easy targets for a different kind of reptile altogether ... the CARNIVORE Cynognathus.

And, unlike most of the animals that had appeared on Earth so far, Cynognathus may have been *warm-blooded*, as MAMMALS are. In fact, millions of years later, its relatives *were* the first mammals.

Warm-blooded, cold-blooded – what's the difference?

Calling an animal *cold-blooded* doesn't mean that its blood really *is* cold — just that it can't heat up its own body by itself.

Cold-blooded animals use the heat of the Sun to warm their bodies, so they tend to be the same temperature as the air or water around them.

HEY! BET MY BLOOD IS WARMER THAN YOURS!

All animals need some heat in their bodies to survive. How much varies from animal to animal. But in general, the warmer an animal's body is the faster it can move, and the colder it is the slower it moves.

I NEVER THOUGHT YOU WERE COLD.

YOU DON'T LOOK VERY WARM TO ME.

Lots of animals are cold-blooded — fish, insects, amphibians and reptiles.

But BIRDS and mammals (including us) are all *warm-blooded*.

Warm-blooded animals heat their own bodies by burning the fuel they get from food. This means that they need to eat much, much more than cold-blooded animals. ✳

I JUST *LOVE* BEING WARM-BLOODED!

✳ A warm-blooded animal might eat as much as eight times more than a cold-blooded animal of the same size.

Having to search for food all the time takes up a lot of energy, but there are good things about being warm-blooded, too.

SAME AGE AS YOU.

HOW OLD ARE YOU?

Warm-blooded animals can hunt for food at night since they don't rely on the Sun for their body heat. They often grow up faster than cold-blooded animals, too.

Before mammals and birds arrived, all animals were probably cold-blooded.

And where do DINOSAURS fit in?

Well, the dinosaurs were reptiles so some people think they *must* have been cold-blooded. Others argue that some dinosaurs were so fast they *had* to be warm-blooded.

The most likely answer is that they were both — some (mostly herbivores) were cold-blooded, and others (mostly carnivores) were warm-blooded.

NEVER WORRIED ME!

ME, NEITHER!

So ... on with the story! By about 220 million years ago, the first true mammals had appeared. Not that you'd have noticed them. They were little mouselike things that scurried about in the undergrowth, feeding on insects and trying to avoid getting eaten themselves.

And that's pretty much where they stayed for the next 150 million years or so, because in the meantime a new group of reptiles was busy taking over the world — the *dinosaurs* (which means "terrible reptiles" in Greek).

The earliest dinosaurs we know about were all two-legged, with small arms and clawed hands.

TERRIBLE? WHO SAYS WE'RE TERRIBLE?

They had narrow, beaky jaws with sharp, curved teeth, and although fairly small (most were about the size of a large dog), they were fast on their feet and could bite and tear at their PREY.✳

✳ These two-legged dinosaurs probably chased after lizards and slow-moving herbivores, although they might have been SCAVENGERS as well.

Before long there were plant-eating dinosaurs, too, such as *Plateosaurus* ("flat-reptile"). This was quite a different beast to the speedy little meat-eaters. It was as tall as a *lamp-post* for one thing, and weighed about 4 tonnes (4 tons).

MUNCH! CRUNCH!

Plateosaurus probably walked around on all fours, even though its front "arms" were a lot shorter than its back legs. But it could stand up on its back legs to feed on leafy trees, using its large hands with their clawed thumbs to pull food into its mouth.

Creatures like *Plateosaurus* were just the beginning. Over the next 70 million years, these large herbivores got bigger ... and bigger ... and *bigger!*

By 175 million years ago, the group of dinosaurs known as the sauropods ("reptile feet") had arrived.

There was *Cetiosaurus*, which was 18 m (20 yd.) long and weighed 27 tonnes (30 tons).

Then *Apatosaurus* — 21 m (23 yd.) long and 25 tonnes (28 tons).

WOW! AM I GLAD YOU GUYS AREN'T AROUND TODAY.

Followed by *Brachiosaurus* — 25 m (28 yd.) long and up to 50 tonnes (55 tons) (about as heavy as 15 elephants).

* **FOSSILS** have been found that show that there were dinosaurs even bigger than these. But amazingly, as far as we know, all of these giants hatched out of eggs no bigger than a basketball!

And *Diplodocus* — a lengthy lightweight at 27 m (30 yd.) long but only 12 tonnes (13 tons). *

These enormous creatures were just gigantic *eating* machines. They had to continually fill their huge stomachs with truckloads of food. As herds of them moved across the land, they mowed down acres of forest, leaving flattened plains behind them.

But *big* as they were, even they weren't completely safe from PREDATORS. Ferocious carnivores followed the sauropod herds, waiting to catch a young or sick animal on its own.

RUMBLE!

RUMBLE! RUMBLE!

C'MON, GUYS! WE CAN DO IT!

Allosaurus was half the length of most sauropods. With its gaping jaws and grabbing claws, it might have been able to pull down a medium-sized giant by itself — but it's more likely that it hunted in a *pack*.

Most of the sauropods don't appear to have been good parents.

Unlike other dinosaurs, they didn't bother to cover up their eggs to protect them once they had been laid.

And they didn't stay around to guard the eggs. They just left them behind.

When the eggs hatched, the babies had to make a mad dash for cover. They were a tasty treat for hungry predators, and their only chance of survival lay in hiding out until they grew big enough to join a herd.

For small meat-eating dinosaurs like Ornitholestes, these baby giants were the nearest thing to a free lunch!

Once a sauropod was fully grown, it was usually much too big for most meat-eaters to tackle. But smaller plant-eating dinosaurs weren't so lucky. They had to find other ways of staying off the lunch menu.

One solution was to grow a *thick skin!* Armored dinosaurs arrived around 200 million years ago.

Scelidosaurus, for example, was about waist-high to a human. It would have made an easy target for any attacker — if it hadn't had rows of sharp bony studs all along its back.

For the next 50 million years all kinds of dinosaurs broke out in studs, spikes and thick bony plates.

Stegosaurus ("roof lizard") was about the same size as a bus.

CHEW ON THIS, BUSTER!

✳ Because the plates were upright rather than flat, they wouldn't have been much good as armor. But they could have been used like radiator panels to help Stegosaurus warm up or cool down.

Some of the plates that stuck up from its back stood as high as a table. ✳ But its best defense was its spiked tail. A blow from one of those spikes would have kept most meat-eaters away.

A few small dinosaur-like reptiles took to the air to stay out of trouble.

YEE-HAA! THIS IS THE LIFE!

FLAP! FLAP!

FLAP! FLAP!

Pterosaurs were the first winged reptiles that could really *flap* their wings and *fly*, rather than just glide from tree to tree. They had large heads, short bodies and long wings of thin skin (like a bat's). Some may even have had hairy skin and been warm-blooded.

Before long something else was flapping around in the sky, too. But this animal's wings were covered with *feathers*! It's called Archaeopteryx and it was one of the world's first BIRDS.

EEEK!

For the next 80 million years or so, life went on pretty much as usual.＊

＊ This period of Earth's history, from 142 million years ago to 65 million years ago, is called the Cretaceous.

Laurasia

Gondwana

South

North America

Eurasia

Africa

South America

India

North

South

Australia and Antarctica

The giant continent of Pangaea had already broken up into two smaller ones — Gondwana and Laurasia. Now these were breaking up into even smaller pieces and drifting apart. The continents were beginning to look like they do today.

Different species of plants and animals came and went.

Archelon, a giant turtle the size of a small boat, joined the carnivorous reptiles in the seas.

And toothy, fish-eating seabirds munched and crunched their way along the coasts.

Inland, snakes slithered and pond tortoises paddled. But the most important new arrivals were the FLOWERING PLANTS!

Flowers make POLLEN and a sugary juice called nectar. Insects just *loved* them! Even some dinosaurs found the new plants tasty.

SO, WHAT IS IT?

BEATS ME!

We're not sure why, but the giant sauropods and the stegosaurs were dying out by this time — along with their biggest enemy, *Allosaurus*. In their place, herds of plant-eating *Iguanodon* roamed the forests and plains.

Iguanodon had big, muscley hind legs and long, powerful arms.

If it was attacked, it most likely ran away. But if it couldn't escape by running, it could use its sharp, spiked thumbs like a pair of daggers to try to fend off its attacker. ✱

✱ Although nothing like the size of the sauropods, Iguanodon was no dwarf, either. It grew to about 10 m (11 yd.) long (nearly as wide as a tennis court) and its hind legs were almost twice as tall as a full-grown person.

But how do we know Iguanodon REALLY looked like this?

Well, to be honest, we don't — not exactly!

But paleontologists (scientists who study fossils) can find out a lot from the bones they dig up, and sometimes dinosaurs leave other clues behind as well.

Fossil *footprints* are made when a dinosaur walks on soft mud that bakes in the sun before being covered by more mud.

Footprints show how big or heavy the dinosaur was and if it walked on four feet or on two.

Sometimes a trail of footprints shows how fast a dinosaur was moving, or if it was being chased by another dinosaur.

And then there's *dino dung!* The dinosaurs dropped mountains of the stuff and, somewhere along the way, some of it became fossilized.

HE SAYS HE'S MAKING HIS MARK ON HISTORY!

Dung fossils are called coprolites. They look like stones or rocks, but they contain bits of chewed plants, seeds or bones that tell us what the dinosaur may have eaten.

Mind you, *finding* fossils is one thing. Figuring out what they mean is something else altogether. Sometimes it takes years and years!

It's a Long Story!

In 1822, Mary Ann Mantell found some fossil teeth and gave them to her husband, Gideon, an English doctor. He thought they were from a giant lizard that looked like an iguana.

Later, a few bones were found as well and, in 1825, Dr. Mantell made a drawing of the creature. He called it *Iguanodon* ("iguana tooth").

AAAGH!

Iguanodon became famous. In 1851, a "life-sized" model was built in a London park. The model is still there today. It shows a big, beefy rhinoceros-like creature, with a spike on its nose.

But, in 1878, an amazing discovery took place. About 30 *Iguanodon* skeletons were dug out of a coal mine in Belgium.

When scientists wired the skeletons together, they could see that *Iguanodon* had a long bony tail and looked nothing like a rhino. They also decided that it walked on two legs, and that the spike on its nose was more likely to be a clawed thumb.

Since then, even more fossils have been found, and now it seems that *Iguanodon* walked about on four legs after all, but could stand and even run on two if necessary.

But this still isn't the end of the story. We don't know for sure what its skin looked like, or what color it was — and maybe we never will.

Iguanodon weren't the only herbivores around, though. Little *Hypsilophodon* huddled in fields of bushy ferns keeping a sharp lookout for any hungry hunter. If they saw one, their only hope was to get out of its way — fast.

Herds of hadrosaurs wandered about with odd-looking crests, like helmets, on the top of their heads. ✳

✳ The crests may have been like "badges," to help members of the same herd recognize each other. They could have blown air through them, too, to make different honking sounds.

Pachycephalosaurs went one better. These "thick-headed reptiles" had skulls that really were as thick as two bricks!

The top of their head was like a built-in crash helmet. When they weren't eating, the males probably spent their time in head-banging contests.

And there was *Sauropelta* ("shielded lizard"). This dinosaur was far too slow to run away. If it was attacked, all it could do was hug the ground and hope its thickly padded back would keep it out of trouble.

HEY, ARE YOU EDIBLE?

NO! GO AWAY!

But for the herbivores of 112 million years ago, there was lots of trouble around. They were being terrorized by gangs of small, savage carnivores.

Deinonychus ("terrible claw") was one of the biggest of these new carnivores. Almost as tall as a man, it probably used its strong hind legs to leap onto its victim's back, clinging on with its clawed hands.

Then it used the huge clawed toe on its feet to slash and cut, while it bit with jaws stuffed with curved teeth.

Few dinosaurs could have fought off a pack of *Deinonychus*, but there was worse to come ...

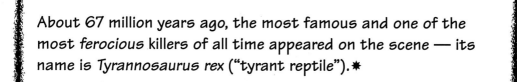

About 67 million years ago, the most famous and one of the most *ferocious* killers of all time appeared on the scene — its name is *Tyrannosaurus rex* ("tyrant reptile"). ✳

✳ The first almost complete skeleton of Tyrannosaurus rex was discovered nearly 100 years ago in 1902. The dinosaur got its name in 1903.

POW!

Tyrannosaurus rex was about 12 m (13 yd.) long and as tall as a two-story building.

It could open its mouth as wide as an armchair, and its teeth were more than 16 cm (6 in.) and as sharp as knives.

But why this fierce beast should have such puny arms, no one really knows.

OKAY! OKAY! I WAS JUST KIDDING!

The only dinosaur around that might have been able to defend itself against *T. rex* was the three-horned *Triceratops*.

Triceratops was the largest of the horned dinosaurs. It was as big as a tank, and its head was almost as long as a full-grown person.

The two horns on its forehead were each as long as a man's arm and sharply pointed. Behind its head, *Triceratops* had a huge, bony shield protecting its neck and shoulders. When it was threatened, it probably lowered its head and used its horns like spears.

Even *T. rex* would steer clear of a charging *Triceratops*!

Then, 65 million years ago, something happened! There was another *mass extinction*.

We're not sure what caused this one, either, but many scientists think it had something to do with an enormous METEORITE hitting the Earth. ✳

✳ In 1992, a huge underground crater was found in Mexico. It seems to have been made about 65 million years ago, and the object that made it must have been at least 10 km (6 mi.) across.

CRASH!

If anything that big crashed into the Earth's crust, it would have sent earthquakes and volcanic explosions rippling around the planet. And it would have thrown up great clouds of dust and chemicals — blocking out the Sun's light and heat.

When the extinction was over, *three-quarters* of the world's plant species had died out along with a *third* of all the animal species on land.

The dinosaurs, the pterosaurs and the giant sea reptiles had *gone* forever. But other reptiles survived. Crocodiles wallowed in the rivers, and snakes still slithered through the undergrowth.

Lots of birds and insects survived, too. And there were plenty of the small, shrewlike mammals.

Nothing to match the size and power of the dinosaurs would ever be seen on Earth again. Before long, the world would be taken over by a very different animal altogether ...

BUT THAT'S ANOTHER STORY!

Dino Dating

The dinosaurs all lived during a period in Earth's history known as the Mesozoic Era (although they weren't all around at the same time, or even in the same places). The Mesozoic Era lasted for about 180 million years. Scientists have divided it into three periods.

MESOZOIC ERA — 245 to 65 (mya) million years ago

TRIASSIC —
245–205 mya
Lots of reptiles on land and in the seas; first frogs and beetles.

THE FIRST DINOSAURS GOT HERE ABOUT 228 MYA.

SO DID THE FIRST MAMMALS.

JURASSIC —
205–142 mya
Giant sauropods; meat-eaters, like *Allosaurus*; pterosaurs and first birds.

OH, YEAH! WELL-ARMORED DINOS WERE HERE 200 MYA.

CRETACEOUS —
142–65 mya
First flowering plants; lots of herbivores, like *Iguanodon* and *Triceratops*; big carnivores, like *Tyrannosaurus rex*.

I NEVER TALK WITH MY MOUTH FULL!

Well, whaddya know!

So far, scientists have found and named about 1300 different species of dinosaur, and they're discovering more all the time.

The first dinosaur to get a name was *Megalosaurus* ("giant lizard") in 1824.

The word "dinosaur" was used for the very first time in 1841 by a famous English paleontologist named Sir Richard Owen.

The youngest person to date to find a fossil from dinosaur times was 11-year-old Mary Anning. She found the first fossil ichthyosaur in 1810.

Are the Dinosaurs Dead?

Well, most scientists don't think so. They think that the first bird, Archaeopteryx, is the link that shows that birds and dinosaurs are related.

Archaeopteryx had wings, feathers and two clawed feet, as birds do today.

But it also had a full set of sharp teeth, three claws on each wing and a long, bony tail.

In fact, if you took its feathers away and put it next to a small, two-legged dinosaur like *Compsognathus*, it would be hard to tell the difference.

> SEE, NO FEATHERS. NOW CAN WE BE FRIENDS?

> I JUST KNEW THERE WAS SOMETHING SPECIAL ABOUT ME!

All of which means that if *Archaeopteryx* was a flying dinosaur, then the birds that you see hopping about in your backyard are *flying dinosaurs*, too!

Dino-wars!

Two of the most famous dinosaur hunters ever were the American scientists Edward Cope and Othniel Marsh.

These two men were so fiercely jealous of one another that each did his best to outdo the other.

In the last half of the 1800s, both sent teams of men into the "Wild West" to dig for fossils.

The men fought with bad weather, native tribes and even each other to bring back the best bones.

At the end of it all, Marsh had discovered 80 new dinosaurs and Cope 56.

> IT'S MINE!

> NO! IT'S MINE!

Glossary

When you see a word here in CAPITAL LETTERS LIKE THIS, it means that this word has a separate entry of its own where you can find more information.

AMPHIBIANS A group of cold-blooded, backboned animals, most of which live on land as well as in water. Today, amphibians include newts, frogs, toads and salamanders.

ARTHROPODS One of the biggest groups of animals. All arthropods are invertebrates — they have no backbones. They have jointed legs and are usually covered with a hard protective skin, like armor. They include crabs, spiders, scorpions and insects.

humming-bird

eagle

BIRDS A group of warm-blooded animals with backbones. They have two legs with clawed feet, wings, a beak and feathers. Most birds fly, but there are a few that don't, such as penguins, ostriches and kiwis. All birds lay eggs, and most of them build nests and care for their young.

There are about 9000 SPECIES of bird in the world today, ranging from CARNIVORES (or birds of prey) such as eagles, to tiny hummingbirds that drink nectar from flowers.

CARNIVORES The word "carnivore" means flesh-eater, and carnivores all eat other animals. Most carnivores hunt and kill their own food, but some are SCAVENGERS.

CONIFERS A conifer is any kind of plant that carries its egg cells — its seeds — and its POLLEN in hard, woody cones. Most conifers are evergreen trees and do not drop their leaves in winter. The leaves are often thin and needle shaped, and covered with a waxy coating that helps them survive well in dry and cold places.

CONTINENT A continent is a very large piece of land that is completely or almost completely surrounded by sea. There are six continents on Earth today — Africa, Antarctica, Australia, Eurasia (Europe and Asia), North America and South America.

FLOWERING PLANTS These plants produce flowers to carry their POLLEN and their egg cells. The flowers attract insects that take some pollen away, but also leave some behind to pollinate the egg cells. The egg cells then become seeds and the flower grows into a fruit to protect the seeds inside it.

There are over 250 000 SPECIES of flowering plant, including roses, potatoes, pears, rice and rubber trees.

FOSSILS A fossil is the leftover remains of a living thing. It might be part of the body of an animal or a plant, or even of a tiny bacteria. Or it might be something an animal left behind, like its droppings or the shape of its footprint.

Fossils may be millions of years old. Usually they have been turned to stone and are found buried in rock. But fossils can also be found inside amber. Amber is the hardened juice or resin produced by some trees.

HERBIVORES Herbivores are animals that eat plants. Some kinds of animals eat both plants and other animals and are known as "omnivores." Humans are mostly omnivores.

duckbilled platypus

MAMMALS A group of warm-blooded, backboned animals with hairy skin that produce milk to feed to their young.

A few mammals, such as the duck-billed platypus, lay eggs, but most give birth to live young. Mammals include kangaroos, cows, leopards, whales, mice and humans.

METEORITES A meteorite is a meteoroid (a lump of rock and metal) that lands on Earth. Meteoroids travel around the Sun. Most of them are fairly small, and if they do come near to Earth, they usually burn up in the atmosphere that surrounds our planet. Occasionally, a meteoroid is big enough to pass through the atmosphere and crash into Earth — then it is called a meteorite.

MOLLUSKS A group of soft-bodied animals without backbones that usually have some kind of shell. Mollusks include mussels, clams, oysters and snails, but also slugs, octopuses and squid.

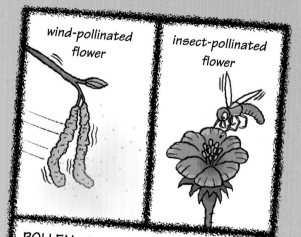

wind-pollinated flower

insect-pollinated flower

POLLEN The male cells that many plants produce to fertilize (mix with) the female egg cells in order to make seeds. The seeds then grow into new plants.

CONIFERS and FLOWERING PLANTS make pollen. Seed-bearing plants may use the wind, insects or animals to carry the pollen to the egg cells.

PREDATORS Animals that kill and eat other animals for food.

PREY Any animal that is killed and eaten as food by something else.

REPTILES A group of cold-blooded animals with backbones that today includes lizards, crocodiles, turtles, tortoises and snakes. Reptiles usually have a waterproof skin and lay eggs with tough, leathery shells.

SCAVENGERS Any living thing that feeds on the dead remains of other living things.

SPECIES A group of animals of the same kind. They look similar and they can breed together to produce young. A barn owl is one species of bird, for example, and a snowy owl is a different species.

Index

Now read on. Don't miss
VOLUME 4:
THE STICK AND
STONE AGE!
Humans arrive – and
discover DIY!